Rhea Wells
Boy of Jonesborough

by Brenda M. G'Fellers

Interior Design by Jeanne G'Fellers

No part of this publication may be reproduced, stored in a retrieval system or transmitted in any form or by any means, electronic, mechanical, photocopying, recording, or otherwise, without written permission of the publisher.

Dedication

To Gary, Jeanne, and Anne – thanks for the encouragement, the readings, and for providing the love and support of a caring family.

And to the late Rhea Wells, a profound and heartfelt thank you.

Acknowledgements

The author expresses appreciation for the agencies that supported this work and generously provided access to the Wells portfolio.

Selected photos were provided by the town of Jonesborough and the Jonesborough Library and were used with permission. The Heritage Alliance provided photos and permission to use those.

The image of the Jonesborough Library was provided by Anne G'Fellers-Mason.

A S A BOY, Rhea Wells lived on a farm in Jonesborough, Tennessee, with his mother, father, and brother. There, he played with his friends, did chores, and went to school.

Rhea loved to draw and sketch animals. A horse was Rhea's favorite animal.

Rhea's mother started a Little Women and Little Men's Club. Every child club member had a nickname from Louisa Mae Alcott's books, *Little Women* and *Little Men*. Rhea was among the first members of the club. Meetings were held in the Wells' family barn, and fireworks once provided the entertainment.

When he was ten, Rhea's family left Jonesborough to move to Alabama.

Rhea returned to Tennessee when he was 18 to attend Maryville College.

He stayed there one year before transferring to study at the Art Institute of Chicago.

In Chicago, Rhea painted self-portraits and other works.

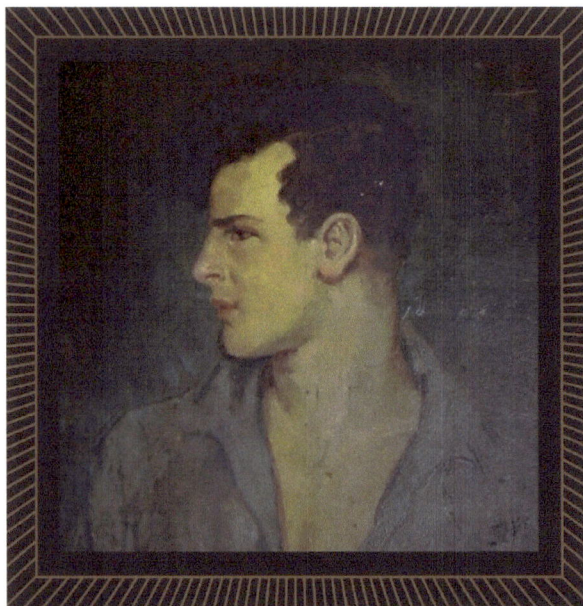

After college, Rhea moved to New York City. He worked in the theatre world, designing costumes and stage sets.

Then, war began in Europe. Rhea and many other young men were called to serve. Soldiers must eat. Rhea worked as a cook in the United States Army.

That European war was later named World War I. After the war, Rhea returned to his life in New York City. There he met a young woman named Mildred Stiebel. She shared his love of theatre, travel, and writing. They were married in 1919.

Rhea and Mildred traveled in Europe and Africa.

When in New York City, he worked in theatre, and Mildred worked as a newspaper writer. They met many interesting people in the theatre world. Among them was Elizabeth Grimball. In 1925, Rhea co-wrote and illustrated his first book, *Costuming a Play*, with his friend Elizabeth. This book is still in use today.

Rhea thought about doing more books, this time for children. He had studied and sketched during his travels and thought he could create children's books.

He reviewed his notes, traveled more, and gathered ideas for children's books.

Rhea returned to New York City, where he began to write and draw.

Peppi the Duck was Rhea's first children's book. It appeared in 1927 and was set in Austria. Peppi was an exuberant duck!

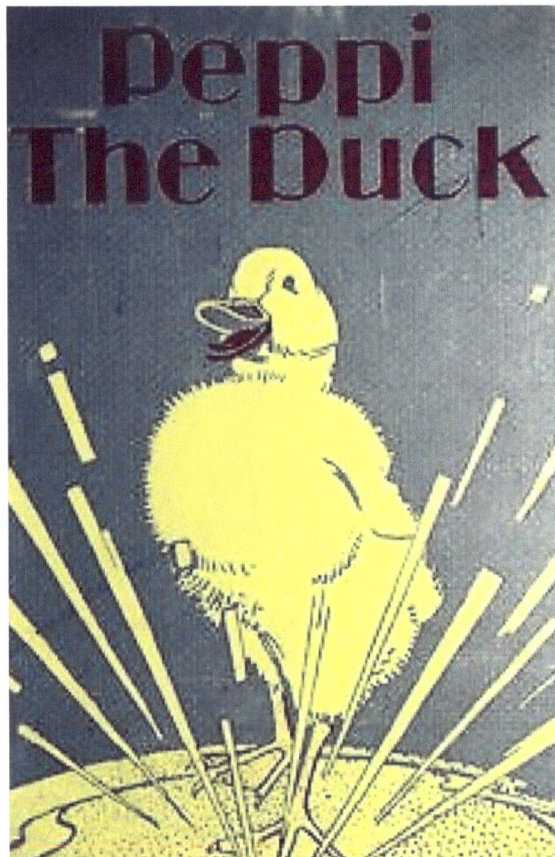

Peppi was selected as a 1927 Best Children's Book.

Next to be published was *An American Farm,* in 1928. In this book, Rhea described his life as a young boy in Jonesborough.

An American Farm received an excellent review in the October 1928 edition of *The Elementary English Review,* a publication of the National Council of Teachers of English.

Rhea found success as an author and as an illustrator of children's books. He illustrated works for other authors, in addition to illustrating his own books.

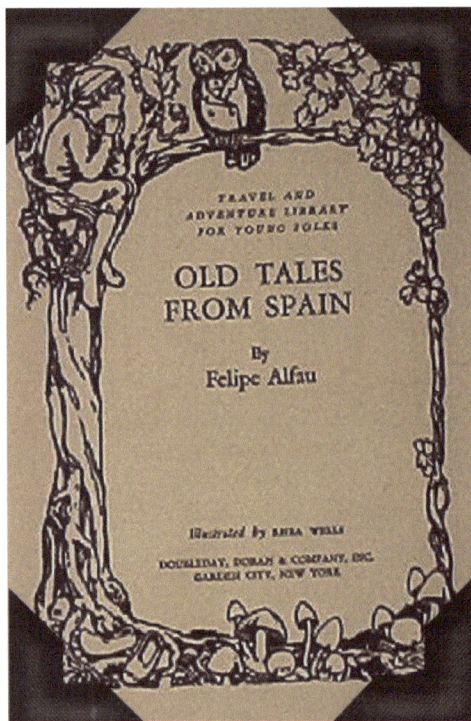

Books he illustrated included *Old Tales from Spain* and a reading textbook, *The New Path to Reading,* book 5, plus several other books.

Rhea continued to write and publish his own works. Titles based in his travels, in addition to Peppi, included *Ali the Camel, Coco the Goat,* and *Beppo the Donkey. Zeke the Raccoon* featured a pet raccoon in an American setting.

Judy, Grits, and Honey joined *An American Farm* as a Jonesborough-based story.

Andy and Polly told of the adventures of a retired sailor and his parrot.

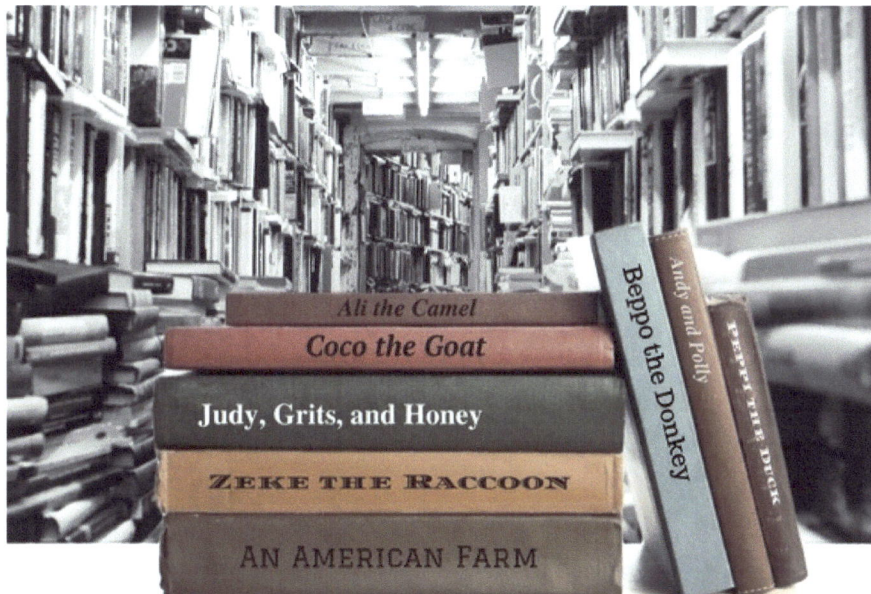

Rhea's books continued to do well in the marketplace.

Rhea loved Jonesborough, the town where he spent his childhood. After Mildred's death, Rhea decided to return to Jonesborough to retire. Upon his return, Rhea first lived in an apartment in the Chester Inn. Today, the Inn is a museum that tells the history of the town. Rhea later moved to a house he built, and then to another house, all in the town he loved.

Rhea used his theatre skills to help organize holiday and other shows for the town.

Rhea also used his literacy (reading and writing) skills. He spoke to college students and school groups to encourage young people to continue to attend school.

When Rhea died, he left his house to the town of Jonesborough for use in children's literacy activities. For a time, the house was used as the town's children's library. Later, the house was sold, and the money used to build a new library for all the citizens of Jonesborough.

Rhea Wells proved that one person, through a life well-lived, can make our world a better place.

Rhea Wells